Remembering
The White House

Emily J. and John S. Salmon

TURNER
PUBLISHING COMPANY

The north facade of the White House was photographed from Pennsylvania Avenue near the end of President James Buchanan's administration, probably in 1860. President James K. Polk had installed the statue of Thomas Jefferson on the North Lawn in 1848; it was moved to the Capitol in 1873. Washington was a city largely Southern in its sympathies, sandwiched between the slaveholding states of Virginia, which seceded from the Union, and Maryland, which almost seceded. Even before president-elect Abraham Lincoln took office in March 1861, rumors of plots to seize or assassinate him and overthrow the government swept the capital. After the bombardment of Fort Sumter in South Carolina in April and the stoning of Massachusetts troops in Baltimore by a secessionist mob the same month, the rumors only grew stronger.

Remembering
The White House

Turner Publishing Company
4507 Charlotte Avenue • Suite 100
Nashville, Tennessee 37209
(615) 255-2665

Remembering the White House

www.turnerpublishing.com

Library of Congress Control Number: 2010926216

ISBN: 978-1-59652-693-8
ISBN-13: 978-1-68336-894-6

Printed in the United States of America

10 11 12 13 14 15 16—0 9 8 7 6 5 4 3 2 1

CONTENTS

Lafayette Park, located across Pennsylvania Avenue from the White House, has long been a popular garden spot and gathering place. Planned as part of the pleasure grounds surrounding the residence, the area was first called "President's Park." It was separated from the White House grounds in 1804 when President Thomas Jefferson had Pennsylvania Avenue cut through, and it became a public park. The park was named in honor of the Marquis de Lafayette in 1824, when the French hero returned to the United States on a tour. This photograph of hyacinths growing in the park was taken about 1906.

Acknowledgments

With the exception of cropping images where needed and touching up imperfections that have accrued over time, no changes have been made to the photographs in this volume. The caliber and clarity of many photographs are limited by the technology of the day and the ability of the photographer at the time they were made.

This volume, *Remembering the White House,* is the result of the cooperation and efforts of many individuals and organizations. It is with great thanks that we acknowledge the valuable contribution of the following for their generous support:

Franklin D. Roosevelt Presidential Library
Harry S. Truman Library
John F. Kennedy Presidential Library and Museum
Lyndon Baines Johnson Library and Museum
Nixon Presidential Library and Museum
Library of Congress
National Archives and Records Administration

PREFACE

"It is the most famous and highly cherished building in the whole country. . . . Indeed the White House is a shrine, not only because it houses the Chief Executive of the Nation but for what it represents in the hearts of the people." So wrote Secretary of the Interior Harold L. Ickes to President Harry S. Truman in 1946, when plans were announced to enlarge the West Wing office building. Truman abandoned the plan amid the ensuing furor, when the public (incorrectly) feared that the White House itself would be altered. The outcry reflected the degree to which the White House is a symbol of the nation.

The White House and its grounds constitute an urban estate, sheltering the president and his family. They also serve as an office, an entertainment center, a meeting place, a lecture hall, a parade ground, a helicopter pad, and a magnet for demonstrations. The people who live and work at the White House are so often seen in their official roles that it is easy to forget that they also have private lives and are subject to the same joys and sorrows as the rest of us. People have been buried from the White House, including several presidents and at least one child. Weddings have been held there, and children have grown up there, gone to school there, and attempted to have something resembling normal lives there. Pomp and circumstance, gossip and intrigue, romance and heartbreak, war and peace, also are parts of the White House story.

The White House itself has had a life as well. It has been burned to the walls once and rebuilt on the inside twice. It has been restored with loving care on the one hand and threatened with demolition on the other. Wings and porticoes have been added to it, the South Portico has been altered, the attic has been raised, the basement has been lowered, and many other changes have taken place that are less visible. Yet through all the alterations, the building has somehow seemed solid and steady, able to accept the changes, adapt to them, and make them a part of its life experience. Perhaps what the White House "represents in the hearts of the people," as Secretary Ickes wrote, is America itself.

This volume contains historic photographs of the White House and many of its occupants taken between the years 1846 and 1971. The images cover most of the presidential administrations between James Knox Polk and Richard M. Nixon. They show official meetings, private moments, instances of tragedy, occasions of happiness, and some of the changes that the White House has undergone. A comprehensive story would require many thousands of photographs and millions of words. We hope that the 130 or so images in this book, along with the captions, will at least give you the flavor of the place and its occupants and encourage you to read more on the subject.

—*Emily J. and John S. Salmon*

This is the earliest-known photograph of the White House, and shows the south front about 1846, during President James K. Polk's administration. The architect of the White House, James Hoban, added the portico in 1824. John Plumbe, a Washington photographer, took the picture, which is a daguerreotype. Plumbe photographed other government buildings in Washington, including the Capitol and the main Post Office.

From Polk to Wilson

(1846–1921)

Known as a penny-farthing, the "high" or "ordinary" bicycle was invented about 1871. The pedals of early bicycles were attached directly to the front wheel; the larger the wheel, the farther the bicycle traveled on a single rotation of the pedals. This model, built for a gentleman and his female passenger, was photographed in front of the south facade of the White House in 1886.

President Benjamin Harrison's son, Russell Harrison, posed in this photograph with his daughter, Marthena Harrison, and his nephew and niece, Benjamin Harrison McKee (known as Baby McKee) and Mary McKee. The goat was called His Whiskers. One day, the story goes, while pulling the children in the cart, His Whiskers bolted through the White House gates and the president himself chased him down.

The oval room on the second floor of the White House has served mostly as a library, study, or family parlor. Frances Benjamin Johnston took this photograph in 1890, when it was furnished as a sitting room or parlor for President Benjamin Harrison and his family. Behind the camera position, windows provide views of the South Lawn and the Mall.

Frances Benjamin Johnston photographed the east corridor or hall on the ground floor of the White House between 1889 and 1906.

Frances Benjamin Johnston photographed these street vendors near the White House during the 1898 Easter Egg Roll. Then as now, food vendors played an important role in serving visitors as well as Washington office workers.

Frances Benjamin Johnston photographed these two children at the 1898 Easter Egg Roll on April 11. An article in the *Washington Post* the next day reported that President and Mrs. McKinley watched the festivities from the South Portico. According to the newspaper, "Thousands upon thousands of eggs were broken on the grass of the White Lot yesterday, not to mention some few that were taken home after the performance was over . . . and as the crowd of youngsters was democratic in the extreme, making no distinction as to race, sex, or previous condition, they mixed it up pretty generally."

Throughout much of the nineteenth century, the public was admitted to the White House grounds and even into the residence itself for a variety of receptions, ceremonies, parades, and special events. One of the most famous or infamous events occurred during President Andrew Jackson's last reception in 1837, when the doors were opened to all comers. A huge and near-riotous crowd roamed uncontrolled through the building, and a giant cheddar-cheese wheel sent to Jackson by an admirer and said to have weighed 1,400 pounds was devoured in the front hall. These visitors, waiting in line at the White House to attend a New Year's Day reception around the turn of the century, appear to be far more sedate.

During the administration of President Theodore Roosevelt, he and his wife, Edith, gave hundreds of dinners, receptions, and parties such as this one on the South Lawn about 1905. Mrs. Roosevelt was a stickler for protocol and made herself the grand dame of Washington society. She held several garden parties each spring beginning in 1903. Most of the women wore white or other light colors, and the participants enjoyed Mrs. Roosevelt's gardens, in which she took great pride. "A White House garden-party in the spring is a pretty sight," a writer noted. "The bright dresses of the ladies, with their gay parasols, and the tents for refreshments, make a pretty and picturesque scene against the background of well-kept lawns."

President Theodore Roosevelt's Executive Office Building, with its spacious and well-lighted offices, was a far more comfortable place for the ever-growing staff to work. This photograph, taken about 1906, shows the employees of the business office at their desks.

Newcomers to Washington who arrive in the middle of the capital's typically hot and humid summer may find it hard to believe that winter will ever come. Usually it even snows several times, as this night scene photographed in 1907 illustrates.

For perhaps the first time in history, the White House was illuminated at night on June 19, 1911—the occasion of the silver wedding anniversary of William Howard Taft and his wife, Helen. Mrs. Taft had decided on a grand illumination of the White House for the 8,000 guests invited to the party, and on June 18, the electric lights were turned on for the president's assessment. He decided there were too few, and strands of lights used to illuminate ships in Norfolk and Annapolis were freighted by rail to Washington the next day. When the lights were turned on again on June 19, the results were breathtaking. The large American flag on the roof was illuminated, and whirling electric fans concealed from view made it wave. Delighted, President Taft ordered the grounds open to the public the next night and the lights turned on again. This photograph shows the fountain and eastern entrance to the White House grounds.

For many years, the northwestern gate shown here after 1913 during President Woodrow Wilson's administration was the principal entrance to the White House grounds from Pennsylvania Avenue. The gate was generally open except at night. During World War I, the White House was closed to the public, and armed guards patrolled the grounds constantly.

This undated photograph, likely taken between 1909 and 1932, shows workmen in a hallway in the executive offices. Routine maintenance was constantly required in the old building, although major alterations tended to be made by new occupants shortly after they moved in. Theodore Roosevelt undertook major repairs in 1902, William Howard Taft expanded the Executive Office Building and added the Oval Office in 1909, and President Woodrow Wilson and his wife, Ellen, made improvements to the family quarters beginning in the summer of 1913.

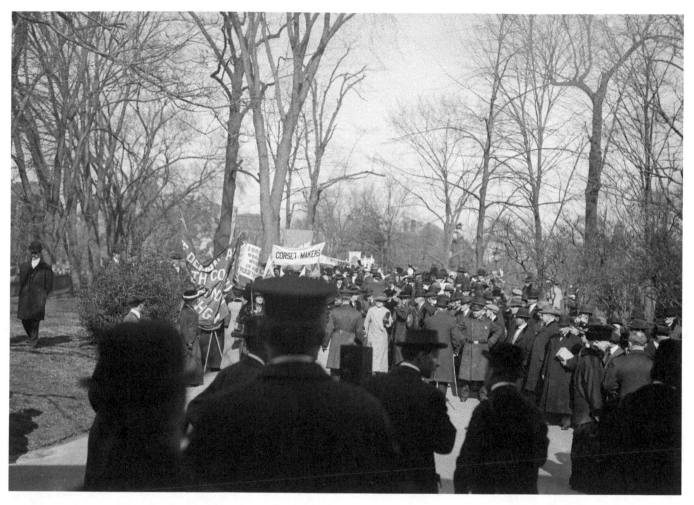

The National American Woman Suffrage Association organized a parade down Pennsylvania Avenue on March 3, 1913, the day before President Woodrow Wilson's inauguration, to promote the campaign for the right of women to vote. Anti-suffrage men attempted to break up the parade, causing a virtual riot. The woman suffrage leaders were not deterred, and in 1914 Alice Paul of the Congressional Union organized a gathering of working women for a march on the White House. Photographed here on February 2, the march took place without incident, and a delegation met with the president, who refused to commit himself or the Democratic Party to the cause of woman suffrage.

Besides lawn parties, Easter Egg Rolls, plays, and concerts, the South Lawn has been used for outdoor pageants and May Day celebrations. This event was photographed sometime between 1909 and 1923.

In April 1918, to set an example of austerity during World War I, President Woodrow Wilson purchased a flock of sheep from farmer William Woodward of Bowie, Maryland. Twelve adult sheep and four lambs were employed as grass-trimmers on the South Lawn of the White House. One of the sheep, unused to city life and frightened by passing automobiles, became nervous and ill but soon recovered. Wool was shorn from several of the adults, packaged into two-pound lots, and auctioned off in each of the states to raise money for the Red Cross. Mrs. Luther H. Jenkins bid $200 for the wool sent to Virginia, and won. By March 1919, the flock had increased in size to 26 and was ready for another shearing.

The Executive Office Building, constructed in 1902 under President Theodore Roosevelt and expanded in 1909 by President William Howard Taft, had a telegraph, or wire, room. The first telegraph room was installed in the White House in 1866, and the first telephones were installed there in 1879. In 1915, the first transcontinental telephone call was made from the Oval Office. These employees were photographed between 1909 and 1932 in the wire room, which was relocated several times in the Executive Office Building.

In addition to the woman suffrage pickets who stood by the Pennsylvania Avenue gates to the White House beginning in January 1917, suffragists held rallies at other points around the building. This assembly, accompanied by a band, took place at the eastern entrance to the grounds.

In 1917, during World War I, three Italian airplanes flew by invitation from Langley Field in Hampton, Virginia, to Washington to demonstrate the possibilities of military flight. On September 22, as reported in the *Washington Post* the next day, "Daring Italian military aviators, in two battle planes of lightning speed, and a giant bombing plane carrying ten passengers, gave official Washington a marvelous example of what the American aviation corps must do to strike Germany through the air." Landing on the Mall near the White House and performing stunts for a crowd there, one of the biplanes, piloted by Lieutenant Ballerini, carried Franklin K. Lane, Jr., son of the Secretary of the Interior, as an observer.

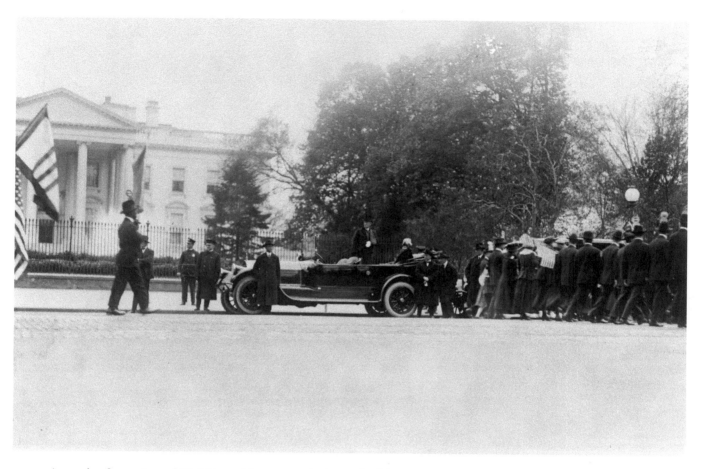

A parade of an estimated 50,000 participants marched past the White House on Pennsylvania Avenue on April 27, 1918, in support of the sale of Liberty Bonds to finance the war. President Woodrow Wilson, standing in an open automobile, and Mrs. Wilson, seated in the car, reviewed the parade as it passed by. Many of the marchers represented government offices, such as the Navy, War, and Interior Departments. Schools, department stores, and banks also took part. The reason for Wilson's left arm being in a sling is not known, although he suffered from ill health, including periodic mini-strokes, that sometimes weakened his arm.

This aerial photograph shows the White House and vicinity in 1919. The State, War, and Navy Building (now called the Eisenhower Executive Office Building) is at bottom left, with the West Wing and White House beyond it. The Treasury Department is just beyond the eastern gate of the White House. At center-left, just north of Pennsylvania Avenue, is Lafayette Park.

President Wilson's famous White House sheep were photographed here at work grazing on the South Lawn on August 29, 1919. On May 7, 1920, the *Washington Post* reported, "President Wilson made preparations yesterday to turn his flock of sheep loose to graze on the front lawn of the White House. Up to this time the flock, which numbers 48, of which 21 are lambs born this spring, have been confined to the rear, which, as a pasture, is fairly well worn out." In August 1920, the sheep were retired from duty; some were sold and others were returned to William Woodward's Maryland farm, their birthplace. By September 30, all were gone, much to the relief of the White House groundskeepers.

On July 18, 1920, Governor James M. Cox of Ohio, Democratic Party nominee for the presidency, and his running mate, Assistant Secretary of the Navy Franklin D. Roosevelt, arrived at the White House to confer with President Woodrow Wilson. Roosevelt is dressed in white slacks and shoes; Cox is standing to the left of Roosevelt. President Wilson had suffered a major stroke on October 3, 1919, which severely disabled him—a fact that was carefully concealed from the public. Cox and Roosevelt lost the general election in a landslide to Warren G. Harding and his running mate, Calvin Coolidge.

From Harding to Coolidge

(1921–1929)

Madame Marie Curie, with her husband, Pierre Curie, conducted the studies and research that led to the isolation of polonium, named after the country of Madame Curie's birth, and radium in 1898. On May 20, 1921, President Warren G. Harding, seen here escorting Madame Curie down the steps to the south grounds of the White House, presented her, on behalf of the women of America who had raised the money, with $100,000 worth of radium for her use in research to find cures for various diseases.

On April 8, 1922, First Lady Florence Kling Harding was photographed trying out a movie camera on the lawn at the White House. A group of women standing in the background watch with amusement. The *Washington Post* recorded the moment but gave no explanation for the circumstances of the event.

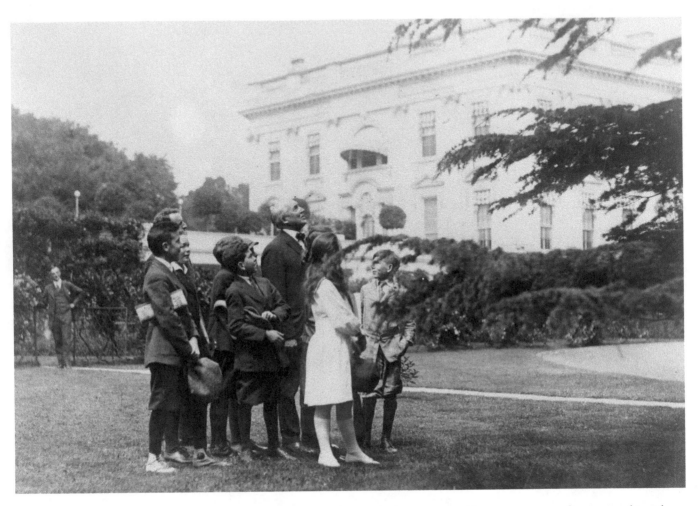

President Warren G. Harding is seen here on the White House lawn pointing out an owls' nest to a group of nature-study students from John Burroughs School in May 1921. The night watchman at the White House had found three young owls, described as "promising rat killers," and notified the president of their presence. The *Washington Post* noted the suggestion had been made that the owls might "grow into an agency for the destruction of all sorts of pests about the White House, but there was no reference to office-seekers." After Harding appointed the children a "jury" to decide their fate, the owls were allowed to remain on the grounds. Fifteen-year-old Jimmie Bradley, foreman of the jury, followed up the verdict by successfully addressing the House Committee on the District of Columbia to "demand continuation of appropriations for nature study in the schools."

On May 9, 1921, after eight years of a Democratic president and a world war, these John Robinson Circus elephants celebrate the return of the Grand Old Party to the White House. Performing a series of "unusual" stunts while passing the White House, the elephants paraded down Pennsylvania Avenue along with camels, horses with "fancy trappings," and cages full of wild animals before a crowd of business and professional people, schoolchildren, and others.

Among the visitors to the White House on December 6, 1921, was the man already regarded as "baseball's greatest hitter," George Herman "Babe" Ruth, who had been traded to the New York Yankees from the Boston Red Sox in 1920 after helping the Red Sox win three World Series. It would take another 86 years for Boston to throw off the "Curse of the Bambino" and win another World Series. During the 1921 season, Ruth set major league records with his totals of 59 home runs, 457 total bases, 171 runs batted in, and 177 runs scored while leading the Yankees to the World Series for the first of seven times that he would do so.

Seen here is a racing car named "The Cootie" and its driver sitting behind the White House sometime in 1922. The term "cootie" had come into the English language during World War I as a reference to body lice, and was derived from the Malay word *kutu* for the dog tick. The British navy had discovered the Malay word and revised it to cootie. In November 1917, the Americans serving in Europe received the new "cootie shirt"—"the latest thing in trench fashions"—which was vermin proof. The cheesecloth fabric had been dipped in creosote, which trapped the lice that could cause typhus. In "honor" of the cootie, a group of veterans organized the Veterans of Foreign Wars' Military Order of the Cootie on September 17, 1920, at a veterans' encampment and gained almost 300 members by the end of the event. On January 20, 1922, Luzern Custer, of Dayton, Ohio, showed off his new "cootie car" in Washington, D.C., and nearly ran over a policeman with his "new demon of the roads." That car was a three-wheeled electric wheelchair that allowed Custer, who was an invalid, to tour Washington and see the sights.

The National Photo Company operated during the administrations of Wilson, Harding, Coolidge, and Hoover, capturing current news events at the White House and the rest of Washington and providing them to its subscribers. This April 15, 1922, image shows the lines of visitors snaking around the executive offices en route to the White House for one of the very popular "public receiving" days.

On Easter Monday, April 17, 1922, between 10,000 and 15,000 people attended the annual Easter Egg Roll at the White House, including 5,000 to 7,000 children. The morning events were only for children, so some little boys "benefited to a considerable extent financially," it was reported, by charging unattached adults a fee to escort them into the grounds. Seen here are the "bright faces of the youngsters" who "made a garden of smiles and color that vied with the magnificent gardens of flowers at the White House."

Shown here at the April 17, 1922, White House Easter Egg Roll is White House Police Force Sergeant James D. McQuade, holding one of the formerly happy Easter-egg rollers whose elders have gone missing. Described as one of the "tragedies" of the event, this disgusted-looking child was among eight youngsters who strayed from their parents and who Sergeant McQuade rounded up during the day. At a previously designated point manned by the good sergeant, the children's families were happily reunited with the "lost and found."

On April 29, 1922, a 37-member "children's crusade," consisting mostly of children younger than 12 and wives and mothers, arrived at the White House hoping to see President Harding and persuade him to release 114 political prisoners still being held for refusing to support the First World War. Several of the protesters, led by Mrs. Kate Richards O'Hare of the American Civil Liberties Union, were allowed to speak instead with the attorney general, who promised to review each case individually and free as many as he could, although he made no firm commitment.

On October 11, 1922, a contingent of 40 European world war veterans from seven Allied countries stopped in Washington en route to the American Legion Convention in New Orleans. The activities planned for them in the capital included a reception in the president's room at Union Station, a pilgrimage to the Tomb of the Unknown Soldier, a dinner at the Racquet Club hosted by the District Legion, and a reception at the White House, seen here in the East Room, with President Harding.

On June 6, 1923, President and Mrs. Harding entertained four temples of Ohio Shriners on the South Lawn of the White House. Seen here with President Harding are members of the Aladdin Shrine, of which Harding was a member. The bands the temples brought with them entertained Harding and his wife. Mrs. Harding called on one member of the Aladdins, the famous baritone Jack Richards, to sing "Honeymoon Time," followed by "My Hero," as "she looked admiringly at her husband," the press reported.

In April 1923, for the second year in a row, Florence Kling Harding opened the "backyard" of the White House to the children of Washington for the annual Easter Egg Roll. All were invited, from the poorest sections of Washington to the richest. President Harding had given a speech in 1921 in Birmingham, Alabama, advocating civil rights for every American, including African Americans. Even during a time of racial segregation, children black and white could join together at the White House to enjoy a day of "tossing painted eggs to each other or frolicking in the sunny spots at their games."

More than 5,000 children along with their parents, friends, or nurses crowded the South Lawn of the White House to participate in the annual Easter Egg Roll in 1923. Adults who tried to get in without having children younger than 10 years old in tow were turned away, though some made it through by pretending to accompany passing children who were not their own. In the afternoon the Marine Band entertained the throngs.

Nine-year-old Warren Sonnemann proudly displays the prize Easter basket that he won at the annual White House Easter Egg Roll on April 2, 1923. He and his parents lived on North Carolina Avenue in Southeast Washington.

As part of the festivities planned for thousands of visiting Shriners in Washington on June 4, 1923, a rodeo of 150 American Indians and 24 cowboys and cowgirls paraded from Union Station up Massachusetts Avenue to L Street, and then out to Washington Circle and back down Pennsylvania Avenue, before returning to the show grounds for their performance. Two days earlier, some of the rodeo participants had made a stop at the White House gates, as seen here, and on June 6, they rode up to the east front of the Capitol for photographs.

While the president and First Lady traveled in the West, repairs on the White House began on the day they left. Among the changes being carried out were redecoration of the first and second floors, a new heating plant, and new floors and draperies for the executive offices, where the repair work seen here is being done on July 16, 1923.

During a tour of Alaska, President Harding fell ill and died on August 2, 1923. On August 8, Harding's funeral cortege left the White House for the train trip back to his hometown, Marion, Ohio, where he was laid to rest. The cortege is seen here at the North Portico entrance.

President Calvin Coolidge took the oath of office at his father's home in Plymouth Notch, Vermont, on August 3, 1923, following the death of President Harding. His father, John C. Coolidge, a notary public, also administered the oath of office while Calvin Coolidge held the family Bible. Appearing in the *Washington Post* on August 26, this photograph of the new president at his desk was taken on August 14. The next day, he sat for 10 minutes for 27 still- and motion-picture cameramen before raising his hand "good-naturedly" and telling them, "I think that is enough."

For the Coolidges' first Christmas at the White House, Middlebury College in Vermont sent their native son this 60-foot-tall Christmas tree, which was set up behind the White House. At 5:00 P.M. on December 24, 1923, attended by thousands of citizens, young and old, President Coolidge touched an electric button at the foot of the tree and "turned it into a blaze of glory."

On October 25, 1923, former British prime minister David Lloyd George and his wife and daughter arrived in Washington for a whirlwind tour of the United States capital, where he visited the secretary of state Charles Evans Hughes and then attended a luncheon at the White House with President Coolidge. In the afternoon, Lloyd George had tea with former president Woodrow Wilson, with whom he had labored on the Treaty of Versailles that ended World War I. Seen here are a group of photographers waiting on the steps of the North Portico entrance to the White House for the Lloyd Georges to conclude luncheon with the Coolidges.

An unusual sight rolled by the White House on February 2, 1924, when a house to be used as a headquarters for the Girl Scouts of America was moved past the south grounds. Begun by Juliette Gordon Low in Savannah, Georgia, on March 12, 1912, and based on the Girl Guides that had been organized in England in 1910, the Girl Scouts was incorporated under the laws of the District of Columbia on June 10, 1915. The national headquarters was moved in 1916 to New York but Washington remained a scouting center as well.

Even the White House in the 1920s was not immune to automobile accidents. This one was photographed on June 3, 1924. If that is the driver standing behind the auto at the gate's entrance, he seems curiously unaffected by the wreck and looks as though he is waiting for a taxicab to take him away.

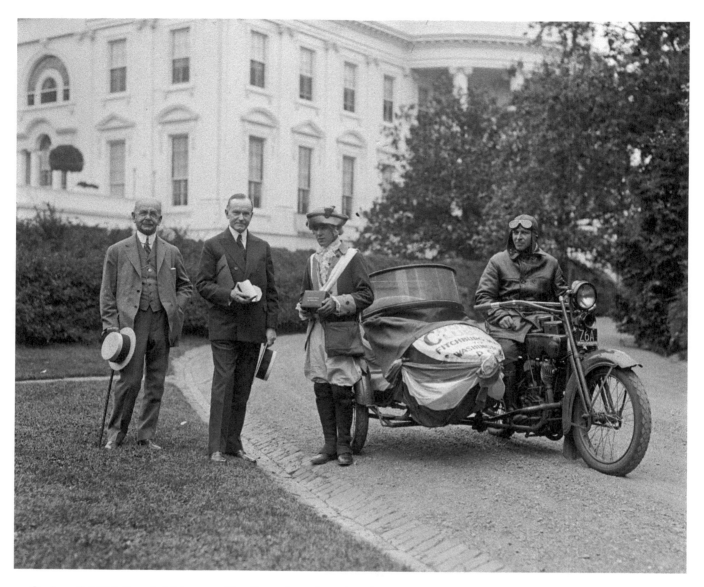

On June 6, 1924, Francis Mahoney, a Boy Scout dressed as a Revolutionary War Minuteman, arrived by sidecar in Washington, D.C. Starting his journey on June 5, Mahoney had ridden from Fitchburg, Massachusetts, to give President Calvin Coolidge a roster of the Fitchburg Coolidge Club's 5,000 members and their endorsement of the president. Many such clubs were formed across the country to support Coolidge in his 1924 election campaign.

In the summer of 1924, King George V and Queen Mary entertained Secretary of State Charles Evans Hughes at Buckingham Palace. When their son the Prince of Wales visited the United States in August, President and Mrs. Coolidge returned the favor by entertaining the future Edward VIII for luncheon at the White House on the thirtieth. The prince drew crowds to the White House, as seen here, hoping for a glimpse of "the most popular man in the world," the *Washington Post* reported.

The date May 21, 1925, was "Tom Mix Day" in Washington, with the cowboy actor appearing first at the White House, as seen here, then as guest of honor at a Mayflower Hotel gala. According to the *Washington Post,* only one guest was absent from the Mayflower gathering: Mix's famous horse, Tony, despite having his own stall roped off in a separate ballroom. To explain the horse's absence, the reporter speculated, "Possibly it was the management of the Mayflower. Probably Tony was indisposed after a hard day's trouping with camera men and kids on his trail."

On April 5, 1926, a record-breaking crowd of 48,105 children and adults swarmed the White House grounds for the annual Easter Egg Roll. Many of them were photographed here on the South Lawn. Because adults not accompanied by children could not gain admittance before three o'clock, some enterprising boys would hire themselves out to be "adopted" by such grownups. One boy had earned almost $5 through repeat adoption before a policeman caught on to his scheme. An adult brought a balloon to the gate and claimed that he had stepped out to buy it for his children. He was allowed in, but others who tried the same trick failed.

The first White House garden party of the 1926 season took place on June 3, with more than 1,000 veterans of the First World War as the guests of honor. General John J. "Black Jack" Pershing, commander of the American Expeditionary Forces who fought with the other Allies in Europe, is seen here standing amid the men and nurses gathered for the occasion. During the afternoon General Pershing held informal receptions with his doughboys and signed autographs for them.

The Louis B. Mayer family—from left: Edith Mayer, Louis B. Mayer, his wife Margaret Mayer, and Irene Mayer—and Assistant Attorney General Mabel Walker Willebrandt were photographed at the White House in February 1927. Mrs. Willebrandt had entertained the Hollywood magnate and his family at the Carlton Hotel on February 1. On December 22, 1925, Mayer's World War I movie *The Big Parade* had been shown to President Coolidge and his wife and son in the East Room at the White House. Guests included cabinet members, congressmen, and MGM representatives, who were entertained by a 23-piece orchestra led by the composer of the incidental music for the movie.

FROM HOOVER TO TRUMAN

(1929–1953)

Workers on February 21, 1929, are shown putting the finishing touches on the reviewing stand in the Court of Honor for Herbert Hoover's inaugural parade. Approximately 200,000 people braved a pelting rain on March 4 to watch the parade with the new president. Umbrella vendors, appearing almost as soon as the rain began, did a land-office business with sales from $1 to $10 and "no questions asked."

On March 5, 1929, the day after President Herbert Hoover was inaugurated, Lou Hoover greeted the Texas Cowboy Band from Simmons College (now Hardin-Simmons University) in Abilene at the White House. The band played first for Mrs. Hoover and later for the president.

More than 200,000 people gathered in Washington to be part of the inauguration of the new president, Herbert Hoover, on March 4, 1929. A day later, Hoover, seen here in the doorway of the White House, made a number of appearances on the lawn to greet well-wishers from throughout the country.

Among those who made the trip to Washington for Hoover's inauguration were descendants of the "first Americans" and of the early French settlers: members of the Sioux Nation from South Dakota and the Evangeline Girls from Louisiana. Chief Spotted Crow of the Sioux is third from the left in this photograph taken on March 5, 1929. The Evangeline Girls represented the Acadians, French settlers driven out of Nova Scotia by the British in 1755. Some made their way to Louisiana, where "Acadian" became "Cajun." In 1847 Henry Wadsworth Longfellow published his *Evangeline: A Tale of Acadie,* a narrative poem that told the fictional story of Evangeline, who wandered for years searching for her lost love after being driven out of Acadia.

The first flowers of spring at the White House appear in this image of the magnolias blooming on March 23, 1929, with the South Portico visible in the background. In the 1830s, President Andrew Jackson planted a magnolia (it died in 1991). It is said that he planted the magnolia in memory of his wife, Rachel Donelson Jackson, who died on December 22, 1828, before Jackson could be inaugurated as president.

Lou Henry Hoover had been involved in the Girl Scout movement since 1917, when Juliette Gordon Low personally recruited her. She then served on the board or as an officer for the rest of her life. For the April 1929 Easter Egg Roll at the White House, Mrs. Hoover introduced a new innovation to the tradition by inviting a group of Girl Scouts to perform a May Pole dance, seen here, for the entertainment.

Officer Bertram E. Snodgrass of the White House police force is shown holding Billy Opossum on May 6, 1929. Billy had recently wandered onto the White House grounds and immediately became a family pet. Soon thereafter Billy became a mascot for Hyattsville High School in Prince George's County, Maryland, and led the school to victory in the soccer, basketball, track, and baseball championships. Writing a note to accompany Billy's return to the White House in June 1929, the managers of the school's athletic association told the president how much the school appreciated "the value of this little animal as a purveyor of good fortune."

On August 27, 1928, the Kellogg-Briand Pact to outlaw war was signed by 15 nations, including Germany. On July 24, 1929, the day that Japan also agreed to the pact, the formal proclamation of the Treaty for the Renunciation of War took place in the East Room of the White House with President Hoover and almost all of the foreign chiefs of mission in Washington in attendance. Hoover is seen here delivering an address to the diplomats, announcing that "the High Contracting Parties solemnly declare in the names of their respective peoples that they condemn recourse to war for the solution of international controversies, and renounce it, as an instrument of national policy in their relations with one another."

President Hoover and his family owned at least nine dogs while they lived at the White House: two police dogs (King Tut and Pat), two fox terriers (Big Ben and Sonnie), a Scotch collie (Glen), an Eskimo dog (Yukon), a wolfhound (Patrick), a Setter (Eaglehurst Gillette), and an elkhound (Weejie). Seen here on September 23, 1929, are Harry Waters with P. E. Allen of the White House police force and five members of the menagerie, including Patrick, the wolfhound, standing at left.

64

Sound movie trucks from Pathé, Paramount, and Fox Movietone News are seen here at the north entrance to the White House on December 26, 1929. The cameramen were undoubtedly covering the Christmas Eve fire's aftermath for their newsreel viewers. Pathé was begun in 1895, Paramount and Movietone News in 1927.

Repair on the president's and his staff's offices and the roof to the West Wing was well under way when this picture was taken on January 15, 1930. Although others wanted the president to have a completely new office building, Hoover overrode them and opted for repairs to the current spaces. By December 26, 1929, two bids for the repairs had already arrived at the White House. The contract for the repairs was given soon after January 3, 1930, to the C. H. Tompkins Company, of Washington, for its low bid of $74,880.

The Airplane Model League of America was founded in September 1927 in conjunction with *American Boy* magazine and in the first year attained a membership of almost 200,000 boys. On April 2, 1928, the first national winners of the National Model Airplane Championship met President Coolidge at the White House. On July 8, 1931, President Hoover met with the winners of that year's contest, which was held at Wright Field in Dayton, Ohio. Seen here at the White House with the president and their winning model airplanes are, left to right, Joseph Ehrhardt of St. Louis, George Lamb of Oakland, Emanuel Feinberg of Detroit, and Steve Klazura of Chicago.

Lou Henry Hoover was photographed with one of her German shepherds standing under an arch of a hedge next to the White House sometime during President Hoover's administration.

This photograph of the George Washington University archers with the White House in the background was made in 1931 by Underwood and Underwood of New York and other locales. Bert and Elmer Underwood had started the business in Ottawa, Canada, in 1880 as stereopticon photographers and moved the business to New York in 1891. After 1920, the firm left stereopticons and concentrated on news photographs, which the company had begun in 1904 and would virtually dominate for another 30 years.

The White House and all of Washington received their first glimpse of the newest and largest naval airship, the *Akron,* when it floated over the city on November 2, 1931, seen here. Larger than New York's Woolworth Building, the *Akron* cost $5.3 million and made the voyage to Washington and back to its air dock at Lakehurst, New Jersey, in 10 hours. As the dirigible flew over Annapolis, Maryland, en route to Washington, it received a 13-gun salute from the United States Naval Academy. President and Mrs. Hoover stood on the White House lawn and watched the *Akron* and its sister ship the *Los Angeles* maneuver over the capital for 20 minutes.

The Workers' Ex-Servicemen's League, a Communist veterans' association located in New York, marched on the White House beginning on October 30, 1931, asking for unemployment insurance and the full payment of the 1924 bonus that Congress had appropriated for returning World War I veterans that was to be redeemed in 1945. These Communist pickets were photographed on November 7, 1931, "kidding" the police in front of the White House. The full contingent of the largely noncommunist Bonus Army, as the petitioning veterans came to be known, did not arrive in Washington until May 1932. When Congress refused to pay the $1,000 bonus early, and the men in turn refused to disperse, Hoover sent General Douglas MacArthur and United States Army troops to disperse them by force.

Governor and Mrs. Franklin D. Roosevelt, who had been attending a governors' conference in Richmond, Virginia, are seen here at the White House on April 28, 1932, to attend a dinner as the guests of President Hoover. Roosevelt, who had contracted polio in 1921, could not walk unassisted, but is shown here with his cane as though he could. As one of the Democratic candidates for the presidency, Roosevelt met with Hoover during his visit to Washington and discussed the world's dangerous economic situation in the face of the Great Depression.

Elected president in November 1932, Franklin D. Roosevelt and his wife, Eleanor Roosevelt, are seen here in the Oval Room in the private second-floor quarters of the White House in 1933, relaxing with their reading. Naval paintings and ship models adorning the wall and mantelpiece attest to the new president's great interest in all things naval. He had served as assistant secretary of the navy under President Woodrow Wilson from 1913 to 1920. President Roosevelt used the room as his study during his administration.

President Roosevelt was photographed in the new Oval Office in 1935. After the West Wing burned in 1929, the original Oval Office was gutted along with most of the rest of the building. Hoover rebuilt it to the same design, but in 1933 Franklin Roosevelt decided to renovate and expand the West Wing further to accommodate more staff members. He moved the Oval Office to the southeastern corner in place of the laundry-drying yard. The new location had better light and provided easier travel back and forth to the residence. Since its completion in 1934, the modern Oval Office has changed very little except in its furnishings. Most presidents have commissioned a new rug and drapes, but two presidents chose not to change the decor: Eisenhower and Carter. Kennedy's new decor was just being installed the day he was assassinated.

President Roosevelt, seated, is seen here shaking hands with Captain Albert F. Hegenberger of the United States Army Air Corps, to whom he was presenting the Collier Air Trophy at the White House on July 22, 1935. Senator William Gibbs McAdoo, president of the National Aeronautic Association, read the citation on the trophy to Captain Hegenberger, who received it for his "work in perfecting radio landing equipment." Hegenberger had used the equipment to make the first blind landing three years earlier. Others photographed with the award-winner and the president are Assistant Postmaster General Harllee Branch, who was in charge of airmail, and Brigadier General Oscar Westover, Major James Doolittle, and Colonel Edgar S. Gorrell, all members of the Bureau of Air Commerce

Democratic senators Tom Connally and Key Pittman are seen here leaving the White House on September 22, 1939, after a conference with 18 other Democratic senators and President Roosevelt. They were discussing a proposed measure for lifting the Arms Embargo Act, thereby allowing the United States to send material to its allies overseas. On September 1, 1939, Adolf Hitler's Wehrmacht and Luftwaffe had invaded Poland, thus precipitating World War II. As an ally of Poland and Great Britain, Roosevelt believed it was of paramount importance for the United States to support its allies, especially Britain, despite a strong insistence on isolationism among much of the Congress and the public.

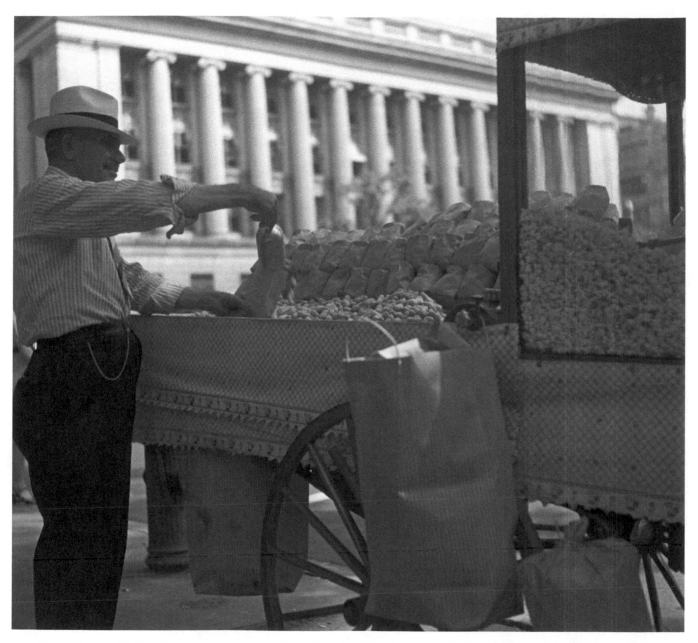

One of Roosevelt's New Deal programs was the Farm Security Administration, which sent photographers all across the United States to record scenes of daily life. Edwin Rosskam, who captured this image of a peanut and popcorn vendor outside the White House in 1940, was one of the photographers.

Eleanor Roosevelt is seen here on Easter Monday, March 25, 1940, with a group of children and their Easter baskets, along with a large flower arrangement. More than 30,000 egg rollers and escorts braved a freezing cold and left the White House gardeners plenty of egg whites and yolks to clean up. As in previous years, enterprising youth hired themselves out as escorts for adults otherwise not allowed in because they were not accompanying children. One youngster offered to get the president's press secretary, Stephen T. Early, through the gates for 10¢. The "hardest luck of the day," however, went to a young lady from Alexandria who was hit on the nose by a thrown Easter egg.

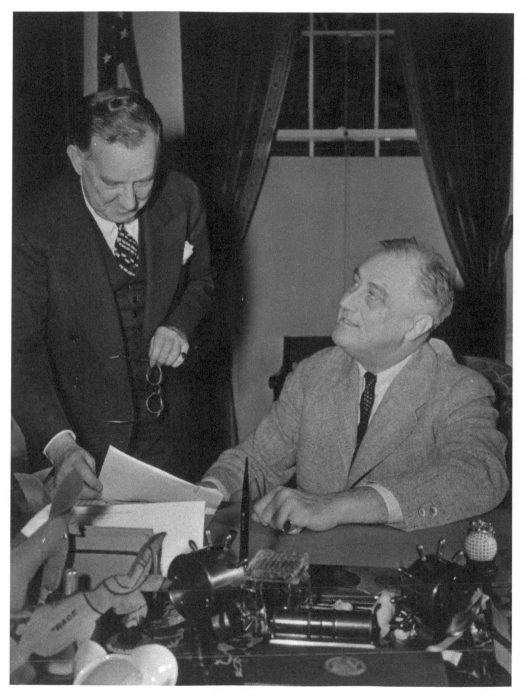

Stephen Early, the press secretary, is seen here briefing President Roosevelt on January 18, 1941. Late in December the president had given a fireside speech describing the United States as the "arsenal of democracy." The Lend-Lease bill for supplying Great Britain with ships and other "defense articles, defense services, and defense information" was being debated in Congress. At the time, England was fighting alone in Europe for survival against Nazi Germany, and suffering through both the Blitzkrieg and U-boat attacks on its merchant and naval fleets, and needed all the help it could get from the United States. Determining that aiding Britain was vital to America's interests, Congress passed the Lend-Lease Act on March 11, 1941.

President Roosevelt is seen here addressing the nation over the radio on September 11, 1941. The United States had just suffered yet another loss of a naval vessel to German U-boats, which were trying to obtain supremacy over the Atlantic Ocean. In reviewing the continuous loss of merchant and naval shipping to the Nazis, Roosevelt told his listeners, "It is time for all Americans, Americans of all the Americas to stop being deluded by the romantic notion that the Americas can go on living happily and peacefully in a Nazi-dominated world." Roosevelt assured his listeners and the world that the United States would not sit idly by and let its naval and merchant ships be destroyed, stating, "From now on, if German or Italian vessels of war enter the waters, the protection of which is necessary for American defense, they do so at their own peril."

President Roosevelt is shown here in 1942 in the Oval Office looking at a globe of the world and contemplating North Africa, where the first strike against Germany was to be made. The invasion of North Africa was planned to relieve pressure on the Russians, to gain French Morocco, Algeria, and Tunisia as a base for enlisting the French colonial empire in the war, to assist the British in destroying Axis forces threatening Egypt and Suez, to open the Mediterranean to Allied shipping, to shorten the route to the Far East, and to prepare the way for further operations against the European Axis. Called Operation Torch, the action began on October 23, 1942, when the British attacked General Erwin Rommel's Afrika Korps at El Alamein. Rommel's forces retreated on November 6, 1942, and the American forces invaded North Africa on November 8.

Seen here in the summer of 1942 is an amateur baseball game on the South Lawn at the White House. The man with his back to the camera is playing in the outfield. The picture was taken by Marjory Collins, another of the FSA's photographers.

Seated on the lawn at the White House on February 24, 1943, are Madame Chiang Kai-shek and Mrs. Roosevelt. Madame Chiang was visiting Washington as "an honor guest" at Mrs. Roosevelt's weekly press conference. During her remarks, Madame Chiang noted that the United States could most aid China by providing materiel, especially ammunition, since President Roosevelt had declared the United States "the arsenal of democracy." During World War II, Chiang Kai-shek's Nationalist government and Mao Zedong's rebel Communists fought separate battles against the occupying Japanese. Until 1941, the Nationalists received equipment from the Soviet Union. America sent troops, pilots, and supplies to the Nationalists by way of the rugged Burma Road, until it was cut by the advancing Japanese army in 1942. Thereafter until 1945, Allied military aid to China had to be flown over the Himalaya Mountains from India.

Franklin D. Roosevelt celebrated an unprecedented fourth inauguration on January 20, 1945. No other president before him had been elected more than twice to the office. Since that time the Twenty-second Amendment to the Constitution, ratified on February 26, 1951, has limited a president to two terms in office. By January 1945, it had become clear that the war in Europe was being won, and the United States was island-hopping toward Japan as well. Roosevelt, however, was in extremely bad health with high blood pressure and atherosclerosis and had only four months to live.

Because of the snow-covered ground and the president's frailty, the 1945 inaugural ceremonies took place at the White House. President Roosevelt delivered a short address on the South Portico and went back into the house, where he almost collapsed into his wheelchair, suffering with chest pains.

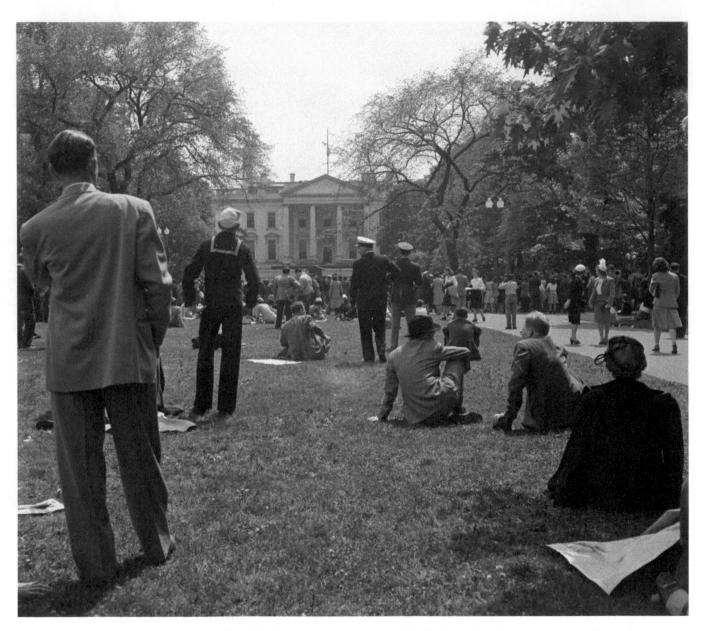

Word spread rapidly across the country that President Franklin D. Roosevelt had died suddenly at his retreat in Warm Springs, Georgia, on April 12, 1945. In Washington, crowds gathered in front of the White House, and stunned citizens wondered what would happen next. Many of them had known no other president and could not imagine anyone else's hand steering the ship of state. Victory in World War II grew closer every day; it seemed grossly unfair that Roosevelt had not lived to see the end.

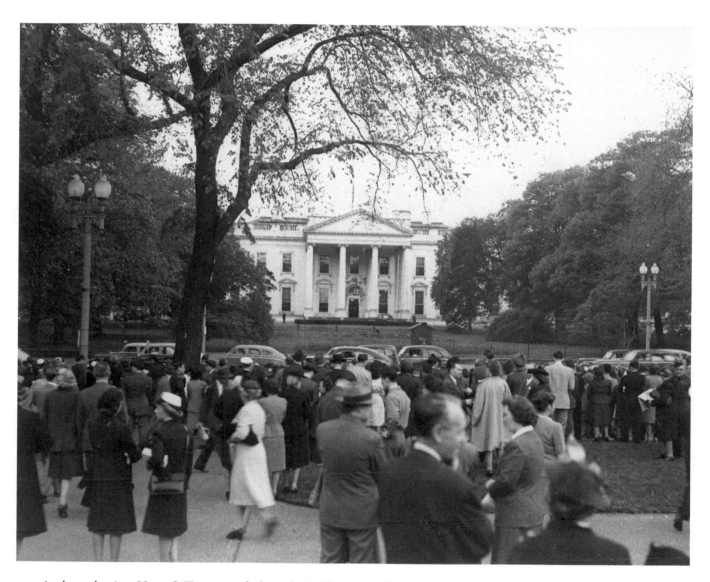

At about the time Harry S. Truman took the oath of office as president at 7:09 P.M. on April 12, 1945, people in the crowd in Lafayette Park expressed their shock and disbelief over Roosevelt's death to each other. To many of them, Truman was a little-known Missouri senator, a virtual nonentity, and they could not imagine him filling Roosevelt's shoes.

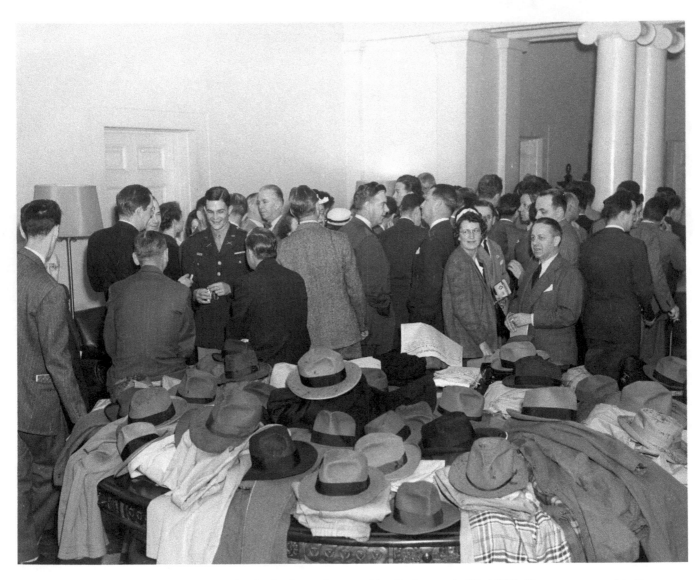

On May 8, 1945, less than a month after the death of President Franklin D. Roosevelt, World War II came to an end in Europe with Germany's unconditional surrender. Celebrations broke out all over the United States, perhaps most famously in New York's Times Square. Here, at the White House, newsmen and other visitors piled their coats and hats on a table as they gathered for the official announcement by President Harry S. Truman.

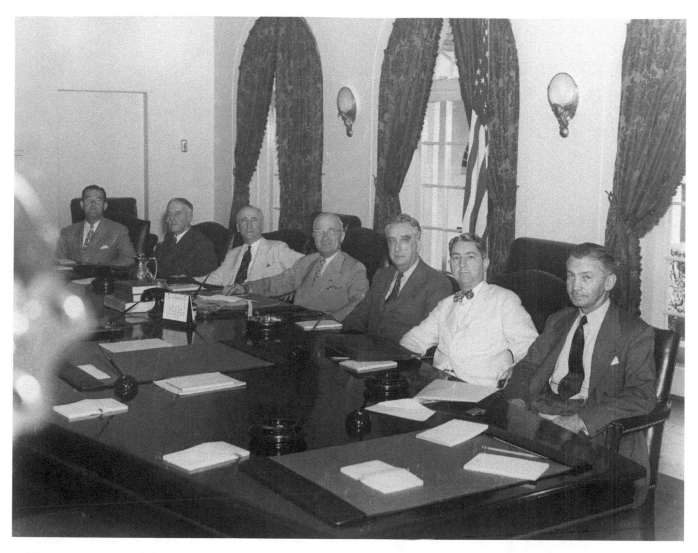

The most controversial decision that President Harry S. Truman made was to drop the newly developed atomic bomb on Japan. Truman was convinced that it would end the war in the Pacific and save American lives. At the time, some military analysts predicted up to a million American casualties if the planned invasion of the main Japanese islands was carried out. The first bomb was dropped on August 6, obliterating the city of Hiroshima. When the Allies' demand for surrender went unanswered, the second bomb was dropped on Nagasaki on August 9. This image shows Truman and his cabinet meeting in the West Wing the next day, August 10, as they awaited word on whether Japan would at last surrender.

President Harry S. Truman announced the surrender of Japan and the end of World War II from the Oval Office on August 14, 1945. Newsreel cameramen and sound technicians set up their equipment in the room beforehand, as this image shows.

The news that America had been waiting to hear through almost four years of bloody war came at last on August 14, 1945. President Truman read a statement to the press assembled in the Oval Office. He began, "I have received this afternoon a message from the Japanese Government in reply to the message forwarded to that Government by the Secretary of State on August 11. I deem this reply a full acceptance of the Potsdam Declaration which specifies the unconditional surrender of Japan. In the reply there is no qualification. Arrangements are now being made for the signing of the surrender terms at the earliest possible moment." World War II was over.

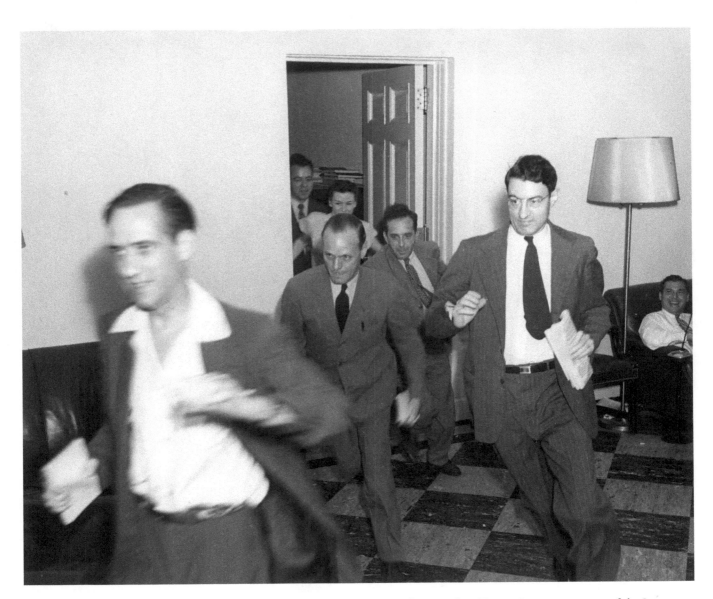

Members of the White House press corps rushed through the West Wing after President Truman's announcement of the Japanese surrender and the end of World War II on August 14, 1945. They were scrambling to pick up copies of the official White House news release and get to their telephones to call their editors.

After news of the end of World War II reached the public, huge crowds filled the streets of Washington, especially on Pennsylvania Avenue in front of the White House. Soldiers, sailors, and civilians jubilantly celebrated into the night.

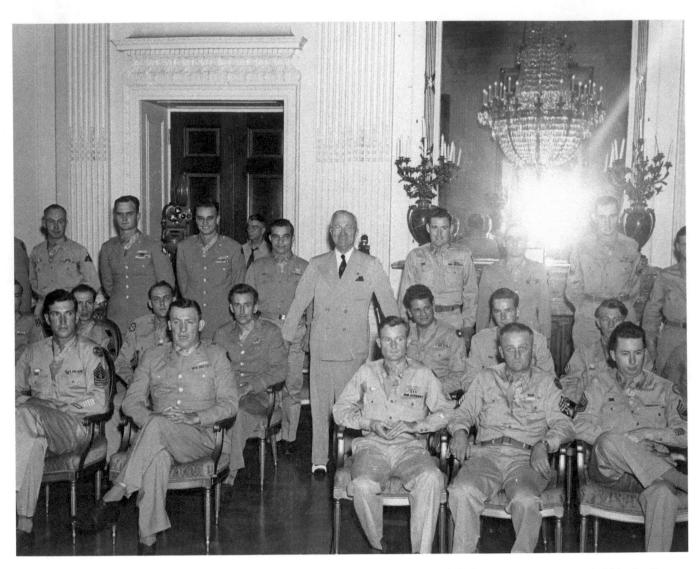

On August 23, 1945, President Harry S. Truman decorated 28 recipients of the Medal of Honor in a ceremony held in the East Room of the White House. Truman, who had fought in France in World War I, greatly admired servicemen and relished such ceremonies. He said it was his favorite presidential duty. Frequently, he would tell recipients of the Medal of Honor, "I would rather have this medal myself than be president."

President Harry S. Truman met with Admiral William F. Halsey when the naval commander returned to the East Coast from the Pacific. The meeting took place in the Oval Office about 4:00 P.M. on Friday, October 19, 1945. Halsey's flag was flying on USS *Missouri* on September 2 in Tokyo Bay when the formal Japanese surrender was signed on board.

During World War II, austerity programs and military necessity required that electricity be conserved. The traditional lighting of the National Community Christmas Tree on the White House grounds was suspended in 1941 for the duration of the war. On December 24, 1945, however, the tree was lit once more. This image shows part of the crowd that assembled for the concert that preceded the lighting ceremony.

On December 24, 1945, the National Community Christmas Tree was illuminated for the first time since 1941. President Truman told the crowd, "This is the Christmas that a war-weary world has prayed for through long and awful years. With peace come joy and gladness. The gloom of the war years fades as once more we light the National Community Christmas Tree. We meet in the spirit of the first Christmas, when the midnight choir sang the hymn of joy: 'Glory to God in the highest, and on earth peace, good will toward men.'"

On July 16, 1946, President Harry S. Truman honored the United States Navy men who had borne the battle of the Pacific in World War II. He awarded Presidential Unit Citations to the crewmen of eight aircraft carriers: *Belleau Wood, Bunker Hill, Cabot, Essex, Hornet, Lexington, San Jacinto,* and *Yorktown.* In his address, Truman said, "It is a very great pleasure to me to have had the privilege of presenting citations to these aircraft carriers. They made remarkable records. When you read those records, you read the history of the war in the Pacific. . . . It is a great pleasure to me to have this privilege today of showing just what the country thinks about the contributions which these men have made to the victory we have just won."

Visiting Washington on October 3, 1949, to open a Library of Congress exhibition on the subject of comics, a group of America's leading comic-strip artists called on President Truman at the White House and presented him with sketches they drew of him on the spot. Among the artists were Milton Caniff *(Steve Canyon)*, George Wunder *(Terry and the Pirates,* which he had taken over from Caniff), Ham Fisher *(Joe Palooka)*, Ken Ernst *(Mary Worth)*, Bill Holman *(Smokey Stover)*, Lank Leonard *(Mickey Finn)*, Ed Reed *(Off the Record)*, and Allen Saunders *(Steve Roper)*. Cartoonists had been accused of corrupting youth, and anti-cartoon groups wanted cartoon strips and comic books banned. Instead, one congressman had a patriotically themed excerpt from *Terry and the Pirates* read into the *Congressional Record.*

President Truman is shown here speaking to a group of foreign journalists in the White House Rose Garden on May 3, 1951. At the time, Truman was embroiled in the controversy surrounding his firing of General Douglas MacArthur, a hero of World War II and Supreme Commander, Allied Powers, in Korea. MacArthur had disobeyed orders repeatedly and defied directions from Truman, the commander in chief. Truman had relieved MacArthur of command on April 11, and the general had returned to the United States, addressed a joint session of Congress, and was being discussed as a possible presidential candidate. Truman professed to be unconcerned by MacArthur's popularity and urged reporters to await the outcome of a congressional investigation, which Truman asserted would prove that the firing was justified.

After about three years of work, a renovated White House was available for President Harry S. Truman to move back into on March 27, 1952. In a brief ceremony, the president received a gold key to the residence, as his wife, Bess Truman, looked on from the doorway. The Trumans had lived at Blair House, on the north side of Lafayette Square, while the work was under way. While there, they had survived an assassination attempt on November 1, 1950, as two Puerto Rican separatists had attempted to shoot their way past guards. Both were killed, and one guard died while another was wounded. Whether at Blair House or the White House, President Truman was frequently alone, as his wife much preferred to remain at their home in Independence, Missouri.

Several busts of President Truman were created during his lifetime, including this one by Nison Tregor, a naturalized American citizen from Russia. Truman posed with the bust in July 1952 in the Cabinet Room.

On November 18, 1952, president-elect Dwight D. Eisenhower paid President Harry S. Truman a visit at the White House and spoke to reporters there. Although Truman respected Eisenhower for his long military career and especially his role in achieving victory during World War II, he had hoped the general would campaign for the presidency as a Democrat and was disappointed when Eisenhower joined the Republican Party. Truman campaigned for the Democratic nominee, Adlai Stevenson, and the relationship between Truman and Eisenhower grew increasingly strained. On Inauguration Day, neither one spoke to the other, and the silence was only broken after a lapse of more than 10 years, at the funeral of President John F. Kennedy. On leaving the burial ceremony at Arlington National Cemetery on November 25, 1963, the two former presidents were compelled to share a limousine, began talking, and reconciled at last.

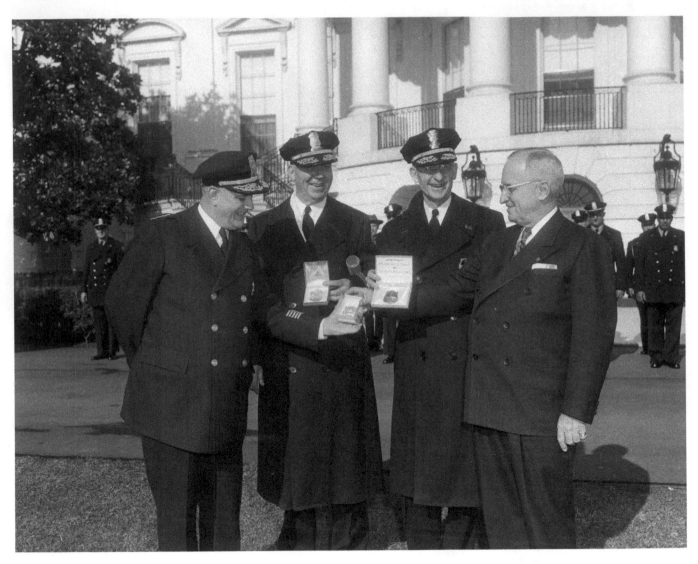

As President Truman prepared to leave the White House for his home in Independence, Missouri, in January 1953, he began making his farewells to the White House staff and to others who had served him there. Most of the men and women under Truman liked and respected him, in part because he was unpretentious and treated them with kindness and common courtesy. In this photograph taken on January 16, Truman is being presented honorary badges from Robert Murray, chief of the Washington Metropolitan Police Department, Mark Raspberry, chief of the United States Park Service, and Hobart Francis, inspector, White House Police.

FROM EISENHOWER TO NIXON

(1953–1973)

Homer Gruenther, assistant to the deputy assistant to President Eisenhower, accepts a Yuletide turkey named Mr. St. Mary's County from Mrs. Lucille Norman of Charlotte Hall, Maryland. She told reporters that she and her husband, Hobart Norman, raised about 12,000 turkeys a year. In the background are two gallons of southern Maryland oysters to accompany the bird. Mr. Gruenther, who was wearing gloves as a precaution, escorted the turkey to White House maitre d' Charles Ficklin. Whether the bird received a holiday reprieve, as has long been the custom with Thanksgiving turkeys presented to the president, is not known.

A noted writer of plays and screenplays, Clare Boothe Luce was also the wife of Henry R. Luce, publisher of *Time* and other magazines. She was an ardent Republican who served two terms in the House of Representatives beginning in 1942. During the 1952 election, she campaigned for Dwight D. Eisenhower, who rewarded her the next year with an appointment as ambassador to Italy. Here on January 6, 1954, during one of her periodic visits to the United States for consultations, she met in the Oval Office with the president, who hosted a luncheon in her honor later that day. Luce resigned two years later because of ill health.

With America at war in 1942, the annual Easter Egg Roll at the White House was canceled and was not resumed until 1953, under President Eisenhower (who had grandchildren, unlike President Truman). This photograph—with Eisenhower at center, holding a child—illustrates the enthusiasm of children and parents alike at the resumption of the Washington tradition. As a newspaper account reported, "An estimated 12,000 persons were milling about on the lawn, shouting and stamping each other's eggs when Mr. Eisenhower appeared with his two grandchildren. Shouting parents tried to propel their children into the President's arms, nearly overpowering a protective escort of secret service men and police."

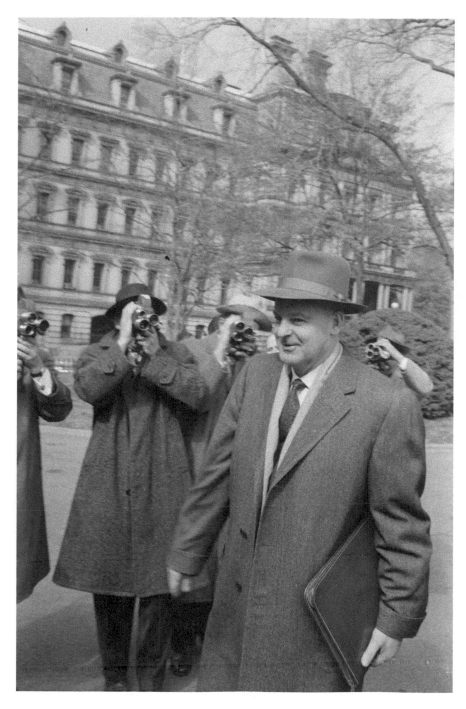

During the cold war, periodic "summit conferences" were held at which leaders of the free world and the Soviet Union discussed issues of importance to both sides, such as nuclear disarmament. Typically, a summit conference occurred only after countless lower-level meetings resolved issues concerning the agenda and other matters. Mikhael A. Menshikov, Soviet ambassador, was photographed on March 3, 1958, as he walked to the White House to meet with President Dwight D. Eisenhower and present the latest Soviet agenda proposals. Secretary of State John Foster Dulles objected to the Soviet agenda as essentially ignoring the points the Western leaders wished to discuss. In the end, no summit conference was held in 1958, but the president hosted Soviet leader Nikita Krushchev at Camp David, Maryland, the next year. A welcome if temporary easing of tensions was the result.

Dwight D. Eisenhower was the first president to use a helicopter, beginning in 1957 with a Bell H-13 Sioux, a bubble-front model with no amenities. In 1958, he was provided the much larger and more comfortable Sikorsky H-34 Choctaw, shown here lifting off from the South Lawn. Other models have replaced the H-34. The helicopter is referred to as Marine One because it belongs to the United States Marines, but the call sign Marine One is used to designate any Marine aircraft carrying the president. Generally, the helicopter is used to transport the president for relatively short distances.

President John F. Kennedy and Vice President Lyndon B. Johnson, photographed with the south front of the White House behind them, were elected on November 8, 1960, and sworn into office in the brilliant sunshine of January 20, 1961. Kennedy's youthful appearance—he was four months shy of his 44th birthday when he was inaugurated—contrasted sharply with the grandfatherly President Dwight D. Eisenhower. Kennedy and his 31-year-old wife, Jacqueline, their daughter, Caroline, and their son, John, brought an air of glamour and vigor to the White House.

Former president Harry S. Truman, on the right, visited President John F. Kennedy in the Oval Office on the morning of January 21, 1961. Truman had attended the president's inauguration the day before. Kennedy looked remarkably fresh, considering that he had not returned to the White House from the inaugural balls and parties until almost 4:00 A.M. and had come to the Oval Office before 9:00 A.M. that morning. Truman arrived an hour later.

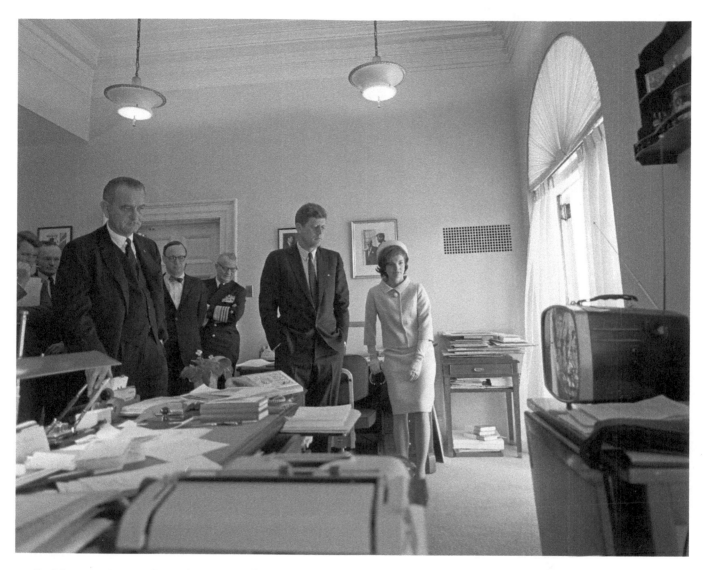

On May 5, 1961, President John F. Kennedy, Jacqueline Kennedy, and Vice President Lyndon B. Johnson gathered in the office of the president's secretary with Attorney General Robert F. Kennedy, presidential advisor McGeorge Bundy, historian Arthur M. Schlesinger, Jr., and Admiral Arleight Burke to watch television coverage of the space flight of Alan B. Shepard, Jr., the first American in space. Shepard attained an altitude of 116 miles in the Freedom 7 capsule and landed safely 302 miles downrange. Afterward, in a May 25 speech to Congress, President Kennedy said, "I believe that this nation should commit itself to achieving the goal, before this decade is out, of landing a man on the Moon and returning him back safely to the earth." As commander of Apollo 14, Shepard would be the fifth man to set foot on the Moon and the first to hit a golf ball there.

Jacqueline Kennedy, appalled at the poor quality of many of the White House furnishings, decided to replace them with historically appropriate and significant pieces befitting the residence of the head of state. She accomplished her goals with private funding, the advice of experts in the fields of antiques and interior design, and the power of her considerable charm to persuade owners of priceless antiques to donate them to the White House. On February 14, 1962, the project was advanced far enough that CBS televised a tour of the White House hosted by Mrs. Kennedy. Approximately a third of America watched the program. As a result of Mrs. Kennedy's efforts, today a number of organizations and foundations, including the White House Historical Association, continue to contribute to the restoration and preservation of the White House. This photograph shows the restored State Dining Room set for a dinner.

On November 1, 1961, President and Mrs. Kennedy gave a dinner for former president Harry S. Truman and his wife, Bess Truman. Afterward, the pianist Eugene List gave a recital in the East Room, and Truman took a turn at the piano to play "The Missouri Waltz," his theme song. President Kennedy is seated next to Bess Truman. List, standing at the right, was an army staff sergeant in Potsdam in 1945 and played for Truman when the president was there to make final peace plans with Churchill and Stalin.

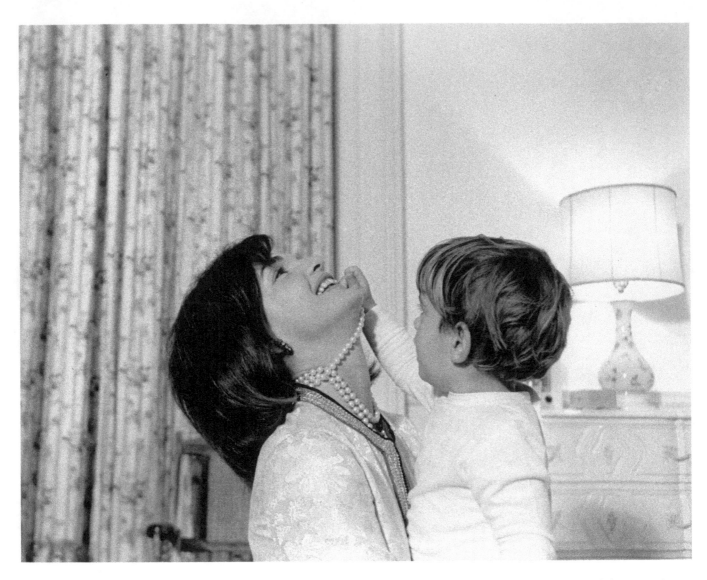

Captain Cecil Stoughton, United States Army Signal Corps, was detailed to the White House at the beginning of the Kennedy administration to serve as the official photographer. He was given unparalleled access not only to the president's daily routine but also to many of the family's private moments. Some of Stoughton's photographs, such as this one from a series taken one evening in August 1962, have become iconic. Jacqueline Kennedy was preparing son John F. Kennedy, Jr., for bed and cuddling him when he began playing with her pearl necklace. Although the boy was called John-John in the press, Mrs. Kennedy later said that she and the president never used that nickname but always called him John.

Jacqueline Kennedy was fond of classical music and ballet; President Kennedy was less interested, but he generally supported his wife's programs. On August 6, 1962, on the South Lawn of the White House, the president welcomed the National High School Symphony Orchestra of the National Music Camp of Interlochen, Michigan. Mrs. Kennedy sponsored and planned the concert and ballet performance that followed.

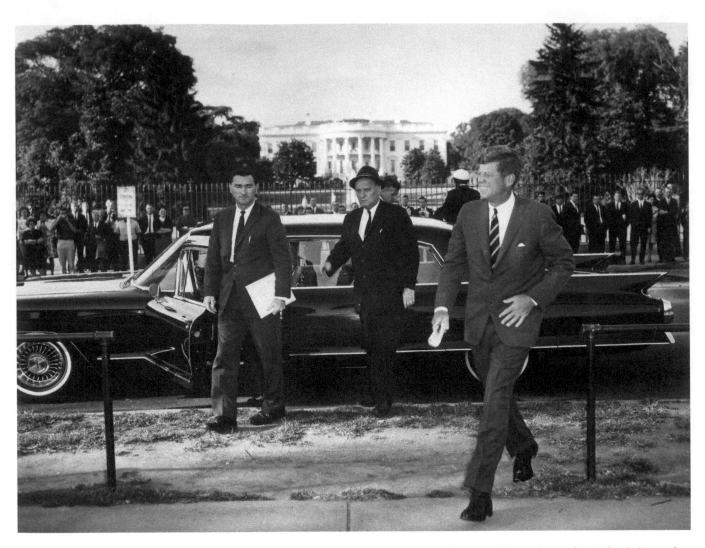

Special assistant Kenneth O'Donnell, Democratic National Committee chairman John M. Bailey, and President John F. Kennedy were photographed in 1962 walking onto the Ellipse, with the south front of the White House in the background. O'Donnell, a longtime friend and political associate of Kennedy, was part of the team of Boston politicos nicknamed the Irish Mafia. Bailey, who first met Kennedy in 1952, served as party chairman from 1961 to 1968 and had long backed Kennedy behind the scenes.

While campaigning for the presidency in October 1960, John F. Kennedy addressed students at the University of Michigan and challenged them to dedicate themselves to promoting peace and to helping the people of developing countries around the world. Thus was born the idea of the Peace Corps, which President Kennedy established by executive order on March 1, 1961. He named his brother-in-law, Sargent Shriver, as the first director. More than 180,000 Americans have served in approximately 140 countries since 1961. Kennedy was delighted with the response of young people and made it a point to meet with the volunteers whenever he could, as he is doing here on August 9, 1962, on the South Lawn of the White House.

Cecil Stoughton's most famous photograph of the Kennedy children was taken on October 10, 1962. Having paid a visit to Kennedy's secretary, Evelyn Lincoln, and raided the candy jar on her desk, Caroline and John Kennedy next invaded the Oval Office and started to dance around the room while the president clapped. Stoughton followed them and took 12 pictures, then had them printed right away. Kennedy chose this one as his favorite and had it released to the press; it was soon published worldwide. He later autographed a copy "For Captain Stoughton, who captured beautifully a happy moment at the White House."

Presidents have used the Treaty Room, located on the second floor of the White House, for private meetings and for ceremonies associated with the signing of important treaties. President John F. Kennedy signed the Partial Nuclear Test Ban Treaty there on October 7, 1963. Jacqueline Kennedy had the room decorated in the Victorian manner to resemble the Cabinet Room of President Ulysses S. Grant's administration. The cabinet table is in the foreground. Mrs. Kennedy's decoration survived until the administration of President George H. W. Bush, who had the room painted a light green. Here on June 28, 1962, when the newly decorated room was opened, Senate Minority Leader Everett M. Dirksen stands at left of Mrs. Kennedy, followed by Vice President Lyndon B. Johnson, Senate Majority Leader Mike Mansfield and his wife, Maureen Mansfield, and Archivist of the United States Wayne C. Grover.

Here, President Kennedy is seated at the *Resolute* desk in the Oval Office. HMS *Resolute* was a Royal Navy vessel sent with three others to the Arctic in the 1850s to search for Sir John Franklin's expedition, which had disappeared while attempting to find a Northwest Passage to the Pacific Ocean (and whose members were later discovered to have all perished). *Resolute* became stuck in the ice, was abandoned, and then later broke free and was recovered by an American whaler. Congress had the ship refitted and presented to Queen Victoria in 1856. When *Resolute* was decommissioned in 1879, this desk was made from some of its timbers and presented to President Rutherford B. Hayes in 1880 on behalf of Queen Victoria. Kennedy had the desk brought to the Oval Office from its longtime location on the second floor of the White House because he enjoyed the naval connection.

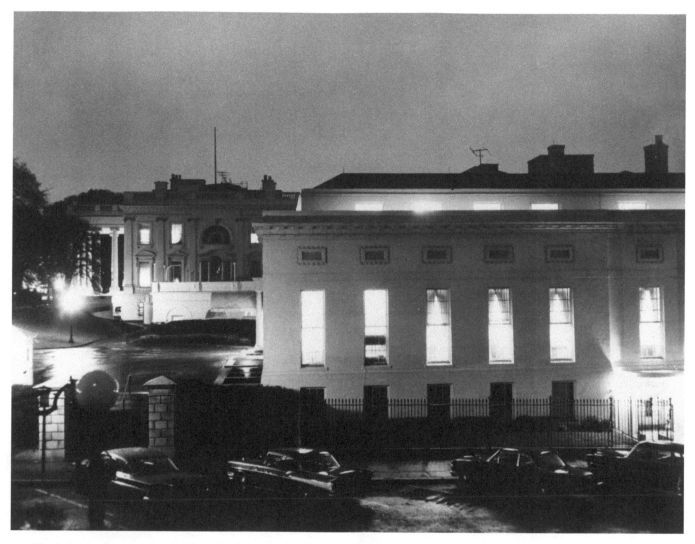

The lights are burning late in the West Wing in this photograph taken during the Cuban missile crisis of October 1962. Soviet premier Nikita Krushchev and the Politburo had authorized the insertion of offensive ballistic missiles in Cuba, in part because of concerns that a United States–led invasion of the island was likely (especially given the botched 1961 invasion at the Bay of Pigs by American-backed anti-Castro Cuban exiles), and in part to balance the large number of American ballistic missiles in Turkey and elsewhere near the Soviet border. After a U-2 spy plane photographed the Cuban missile sites under construction on October 15, Kennedy demanded that the missiles be removed. Krushchev refused, and the crisis escalated for two weeks. Throughout, Kennedy met extensively with key advisors, the Joint Chiefs of Staff, and the cabinet. His secret tape-recordings of those meetings, released by the John F. Kennedy Library in 1997, show how close the world came to nuclear annihilation.

President John F. Kennedy's demands to Soviet premier Nikita Krushchev that offensive missiles discovered in Cuba be removed produced mostly belligerent responses. Kennedy and his advisors studied three options: an air attack on the missile sites, a full-scale military invasion, or a naval blockade or quarantine of Cuba. The Joint Chiefs of Staff advocated for the first two options, but Kennedy supposed that either would invite Soviet nuclear retaliation. He preferred a naval quarantine against offensive weaponry only, one step removed from a general blockade, which in international law is an act of war. On October 23, 1962, as shown in this photograph, Kennedy signed the Proclamation for Interdiction of the Delivery of Offensive Weapons in Cuba. On October 28, Krushchev agreed to remove the missiles from Cuba in exchange for a pledge from the United States not to invade and, secretly, a pledge to remove the American missiles from Turkey. The crisis was over.

On June 22, 1963, President John F. Kennedy met at the White House with 30 civil rights leaders. They included Dr. Martin Luther King, Jr., NAACP executive secretary Roy Wilkins, Congress on Racial Equality leader James Farmer, and United Automobile Workers president Walter Reuther. In this photograph of the delegation outside the White House, King and Wilkins stand at left and right, respectively, of Attorney General Robert F. Kennedy. President Kennedy also met privately with King and Wilkins to ask whether it might be counterproductive to continue holding civil rights demonstrations while Congress was debating his civil rights program. The president was concerned that the demonstrations might further inflame opposition from Southern legislators, but he did not ask that they be canceled. On the same day, he issued Executive Order 11114, which expanded the authority of the President's Committee on Equal Employment Opportunity to include the "withdrawal of Federal funds from construction projects where racial discrimination is practiced."

President Kennedy occasionally invited groups to hold meetings on subjects of national concern in the White House; then he would make an appearance and offer some remarks, as he is shown doing here in the East Room. For example, on May 9, 1963, he addressed a meeting of the Citizens Committee for Tax Reduction and Revision, and on June 11, he spoke to a conference of businessmen about the need to desegregate. Both addresses were given in the East Room.

President John F. Kennedy was assassinated in Dallas on Friday, November 22, 1963. For the next three days, Americans watched on television as one unforgettable scene after another unfolded: the return of Kennedy's body to Washington and Mrs. Kennedy climbing down from Air Force One in her bloodstained suit; the flag-draped casket reposing first in the East Room of the White House and then in the Capitol Rotunda; the murder of the assassin, Lee Harvey Oswald; Kennedy's funeral Mass; the procession, the riderless horse, and the unceasing thump of muffled drums; the burial at Arlington National Cemetery and the bugler breaking a note as he played Taps. Here, on Sunday, November 24, Jacqueline Kennedy and the children are waiting to leave the White House for the Capitol.

Vice-president Lyndon B. Johnson succeeded to the presidency after the assassination of President John F. Kennedy on November 22, 1963. A former senator from Texas, Johnson steered some important pieces of legislation through the Congress, most significantly the Civil Rights Act of 1964. He also mired the United States deeper in an increasingly unpopular war in Vietnam. Several of Kennedy's former aides have asserted that Kennedy would have removed the small number of American advisors he sent there if he had lived and in 1964 been reelected, although Kennedy himself made no definitive statement. President Johnson did, however, "escalate" America's role in the conflict, adding huge numbers of combat troops. Here, Johnson is walking on the White House lawn with the Joint Chiefs of Staff on April 8, 1965.

McGeorge "Mac" Bundy and President Johnson were photographed on August 23, 1967, during a meeting in the Oval Office. Bundy had come to Washington with President Kennedy in 1961, and had served as National Security Advisor to Kennedy and then to Johnson until Bundy left government in 1966. He served as president of the Ford Foundation from then until 1979. At the time of this meeting, he was also serving as chairman of the Special Presidential Committee on the Middle East. He reported to the president on the Middle East crisis, also known as the Six-Day War, in which Israel fought and defeated Egypt, Syria, and Jordan in June 1967.

Richard M. Nixon, who had lost to John F. Kennedy in the 1960 presidential election, defeated Hubert H. Humphrey in the 1968 election. Nixon alleged that he had a "secret plan" to end the war in Vietnam; after he took office he began searching for a way out of the quagmire. In June 1969, he flew to Midway Island to meet with South Vietnam President Nguyen Van Thieu. On his way back to Washington, he stopped in Honolulu and was briefed on other issues in the Pacific from several commanders including Admiral John S. McCain. When Nixon returned to the White House on June 10, he was met by a group of well-wishers including his daughter Tricia, Vice President Spiro T. Agnew, and Pat Nixon, the president's wife, all shown here. Nixon gave a short report on his trip, and later announced that 25,000 American troops would be withdrawn from Vietnam.

Notes on the Photographs

These notes, listed by page number, attempt to include all aspects known of the photographs. Each of the photographs is identified by the page number, a title or description, photographer and collection, archive, and call or box number when applicable. Although every attempt was made to collect all data, in some cases complete data may have been unavailable due to the age and condition of some of the photographs and records.

ii **The North Facade of the White House**
Library of Congress
LC-DIG-npcc-19925

vi **Lafayette Park**
Library of Congress
LC-USZ62-117991

x **Earliest-known Photo of the White House**
Library of Congress
LC-USZ62-112293
Photo by John Plumbe

2 **High Bicycle**
National Archives and Records Administration
77-RP-73474

3 **Russell Harrison, Son of President Harrison**
Library of Congress
LC-USZ62-118058
Photo by Frances Benjamin Johnston

4 **The Oval Room**
Library of Congress
LC-USZ62-127424
Photo by Frances Benjamin Johnston

5 **East Corridor on Ground Floor**
Library of Congress
LC-USZ62-127421
Photo by Frances Benjamin Johnston

6 **Street Vendors near the White House**
Library of Congress
LC-USZ62-94133
Photo by Frances Benjamin Johnston

7 **Two Children at the 1898 Easter Egg Roll**
Library of Congress
LC-USZ62-46453
Photo by Frances Benjamin Johnston

8 **The Public Visiting the White House**
Library of Congress
LC-USZ62-94542

9 **White House Garden Party**
Library of Congress
LC-USZ62-126408

10 **Employees of the Business Office**
Library of Congress
LC-USZ62-131523
Photo by Waldon Fawcett

11 **Snowy Night at the White House**
Library of Congress
LC-USZ62-91031

12 **White House Illuminated at Night**
Library of Congress
LC-DIG-ggbain-09352

13 **The Northwestern Gate to the White House**
Library of Congress
LC-USZ62-131622

14 **Workmen in the Hallway of the Executive Office**
Library of Congress
LC-USZ62-127687

15 **Woman Suffrage March**
Library of Congress
LC-DIG-npcc-19207

16 **May Day Celebration on the South Lawn**
Library of Congress
LC-DIG-npcc-18593

17 **White House Sheep**
Library of Congress
LC-USZ62-105733

18 **The Wire Room in the White House**
Library of Congress
LC-USZ62-131522

19 **Rally at the Eastern Entrance**
Library of Congress
LC-USZ62-131914

20 **Italian Airplane**
Library of Congress
LC-DIG-npcc-28120

21 **Parade in Front of the White House**
Library of Congress
LC-USZ62-132057

22 **Aerial Photograph of the White House**
Library of Congress
LC-USZ62-124275

23 **White House Sheep no. 2**
Library of Congress
LC-USZ62-11417

24 **James M. Cox and Franklin D. Roosevelt**
Library of Congress
LC-USZ62-92408

26 **Madame Marie Curie**
Library of Congress
LC-USZ62-2211

27 **First Lady Florence Kling Harding**
Library of Congress
LC-USZ62-132073

28 **President Harding with Nature-study Students**
Library of Congress
LC-USZ62-132071

9 781683 368946